AN OLD-FASHIONED
CHRISTMAS

An Old-Fashioned Christmas

Copyright © 2008 by Patrick Regan. All rights reserved. Printed in Singapore. No part of this book may be used or reproduced in any manner whatsoever without written permission except in the case of reprints in the context of reviews. For information, write Andrews McMeel Publishing, LLC, an Andrews McMeel Universal company, 1130 Walnut Street, Kansas City, Missouri 64106.

08 09 10 11 12 TWP 10 9 8 7 6 5 4 3 2 1

ISBN-13: 978-0-7407-7384-6
ISBN-10: 0-7407-7384-4

Library of Congress Control Number: 2008921096

www.andrewsmcmeel.com

Attention: Schools and Businesses
Andrews McMeel books are available at quantity discounts with bulk purchase for educational, business, or sales promotional use. For information, please write to: Special Sales Department, Andrews McMeel Publishing, LLC, 1130 Walnut Street, Kansas City, Missouri 64106.

AN OLD-FASHIONED
CHRISTMAS

Patrick
REGAN

**Andrews McMeel
Publishing, LLC**

Kansas City

Introduction

Remember Christmas? Old honest-to-goodness, chestnuts-roasting, sugarplums-dancing, round-yon-virgin Christmas? Remember when the glorious strains of *Adeste Fideles* came courtesy of a group of ruddy-cheeked carolers at your door and not from a ringtone somewhere deep in the inflatable front yard snowglobe aisle at Wal-Mart?

Sad to say, those days have melted away like a snowflake on a hobo's eyelash.* Blight took the last chestnut tree years ago, dancing confections have been outlawed in every state but Nevada, and, well, we all know there's no such thing as a virgin anymore.

Thank goodness, then, that we still have photos of those halcyon days of Christmas. From brittle, old snapshots, honest faces look back at us through the decades; they are strangers, but we know them still. Perhaps they remind us of ourselves. Perhaps we drink a little too much.

The point is, we could all use a little reminder of what Christmas is really about: hobos, orphans, boozed-up Santas, pill-popping housewives, and the shattered dreams of adorable children. It's Christmas again—just like you remember it.

* A flaming hobo

Just remember, sweetie, if I see another cookbook under this tree on Christmas morning, the next balls to get hung around here will be yours.

Okay, kid. Gotta put it all back now.
That was just a market research test
to find out what poor, four-year-old orphans
would want for Christmas.

Nobody had to tell Leonard to keep the Yuletide gay.

H obo Santa couldn't even fool the "special needs" toddlers.

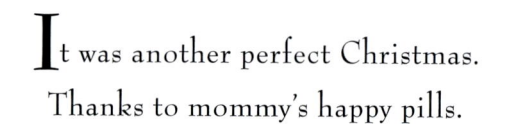

It was another perfect Christmas.
Thanks to mommy's happy pills.

Little Jessica had finally found the dolly
just for her—with beautiful blue eyes,
a perky little nose, and fingernails she could chew
when mommy and daddy were fighting again.

The Ladder Safety Council does not endorse this image (to say nothing of the Fashion Police).

Okay. Back row—*nice* projection. But remember, the audience will be prospective adoptive parents. You don't want them thinking you might eat their cat.

All right, here's the deal. You work on that posture, and Santa will bring you a Raggedy Ann. And you, Big Eyes, on my lap—tell your mom to quit cutting your hair herself. Next!

Kid, you rip one now and *you're* going to be the tree topper.

Mrs. Larson called it the *Annual Larson Family Holiday Hootenanny!* Mr. Larson called it the most effective form of birth control imaginable.

T̲hough the boys at the orphanage didn't seem to notice, Santa could not get the thought out of his head: "Bitch washed my suit with a Kleenex in the pocket *again!*"

Nothing captures the magic of Christmas
like the drooling face of a child
and a cheap-ass, little fake tree.

It's not really whoring

if you do it just for presents!

With the mantle lavishly festooned and the Yule bulb burning in the fireplace, hell, it could have been the little house on the prairie. Of course, it was really Aunt Helen's town house in Jersey City.

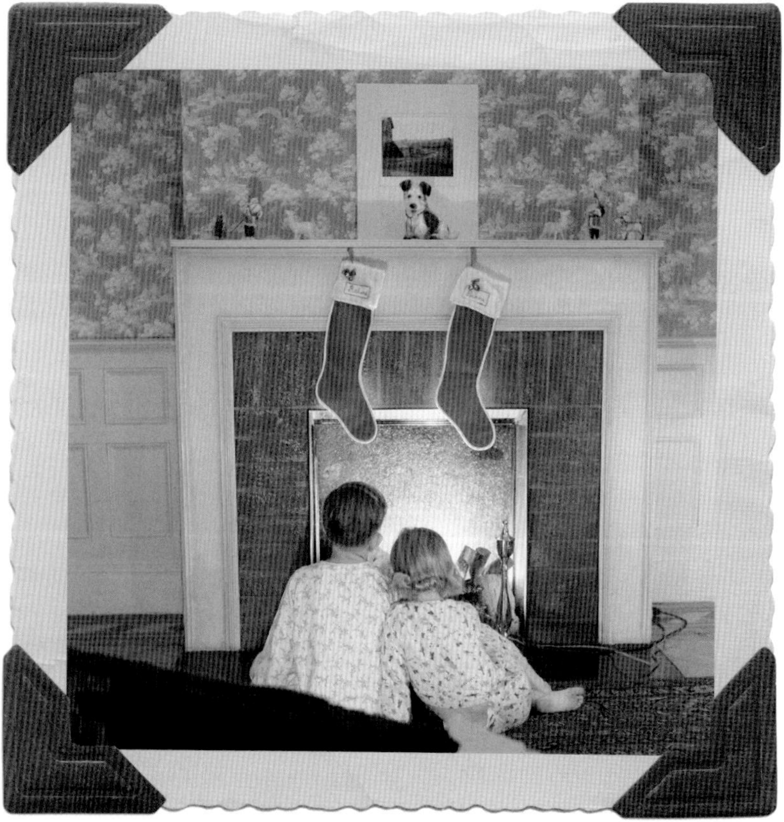

For heaven's sake, honey, just go up with Santa and sit on his lap. He's not going to eat you. At least, I don't *think* he's going to eat you.

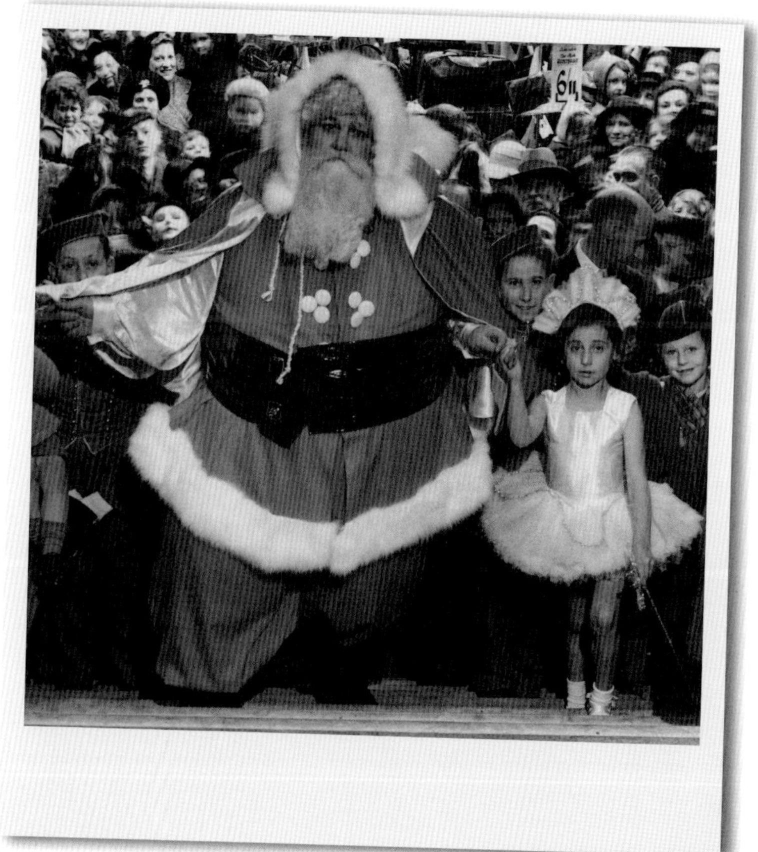

It's the hootch what keeps him jolly.

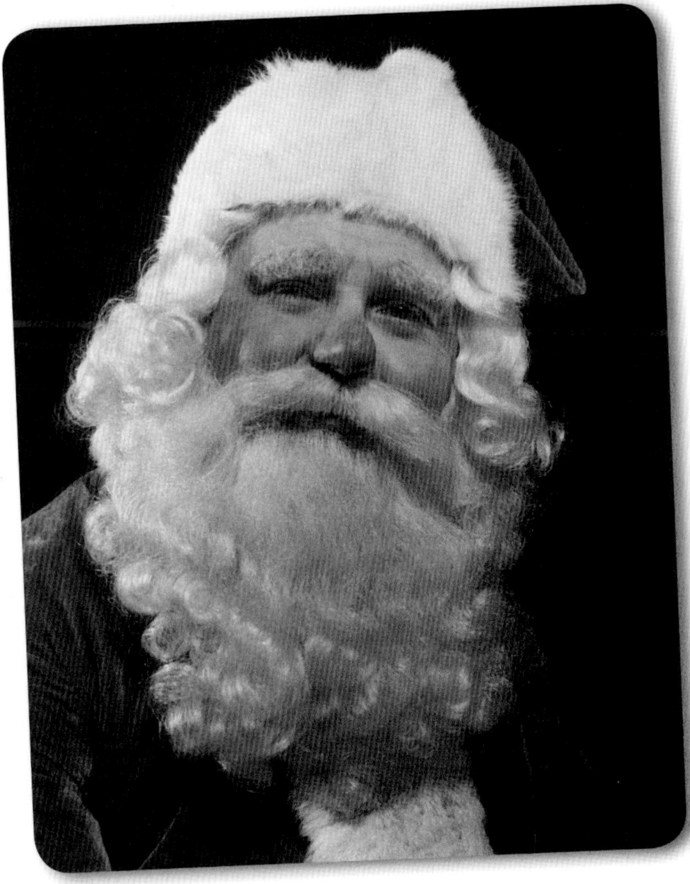

Okay, Santa. We admit the beard is real . . .
but what do you mean "the drapes match the carpet"?

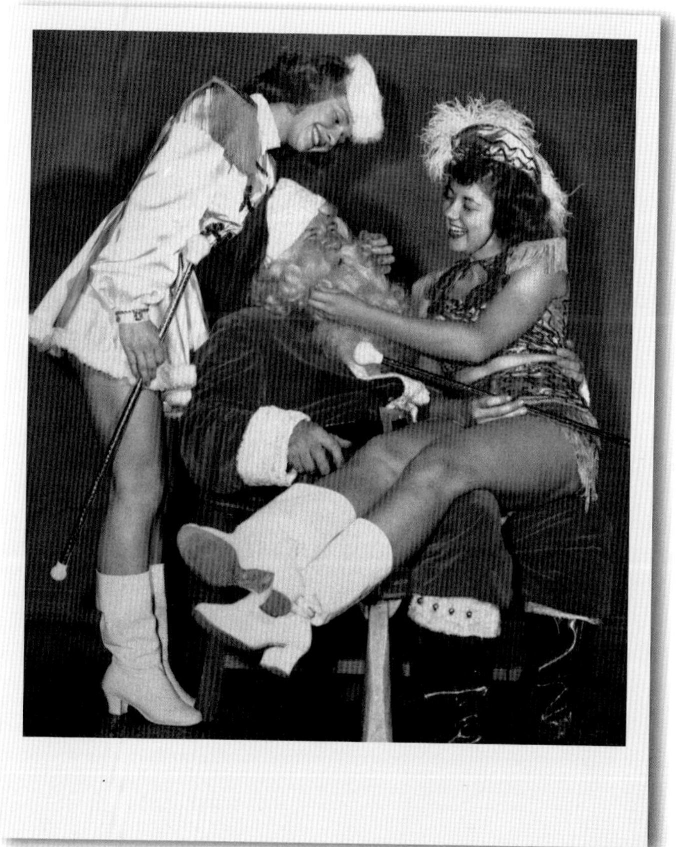

Letter from home, Private. From your wife. Says don't worry about anything because your brother came over and helped trim her tree. Says he trimmed it real nice. Well, Merry Christmas, Private.

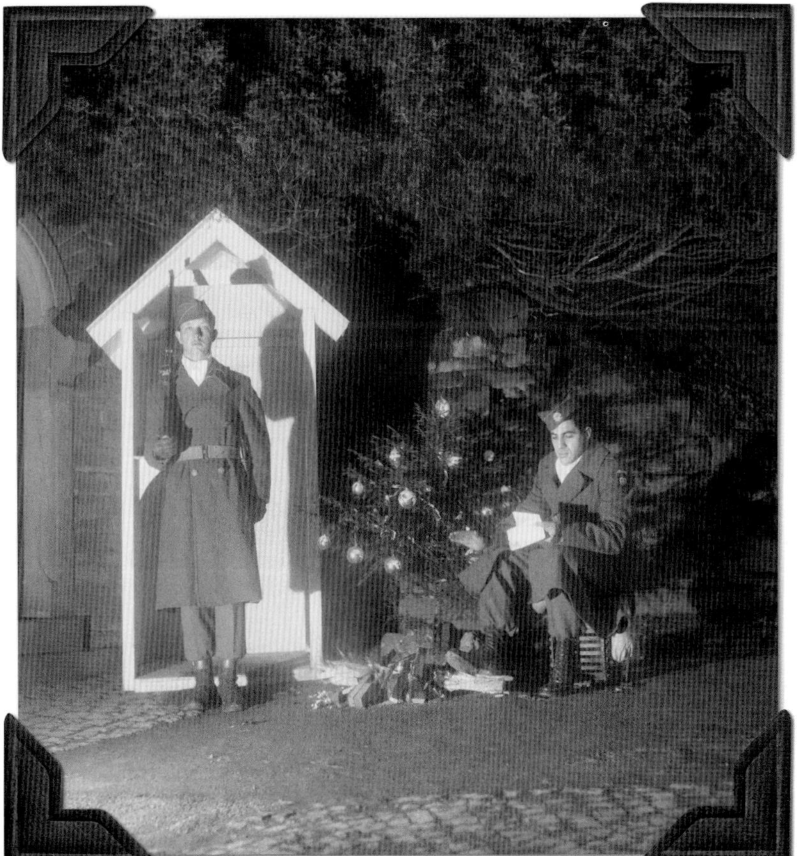

Nobody was gonna sleep in heavenly peace as long as "Tiny Itzhak" was sawing away on that fiddle.

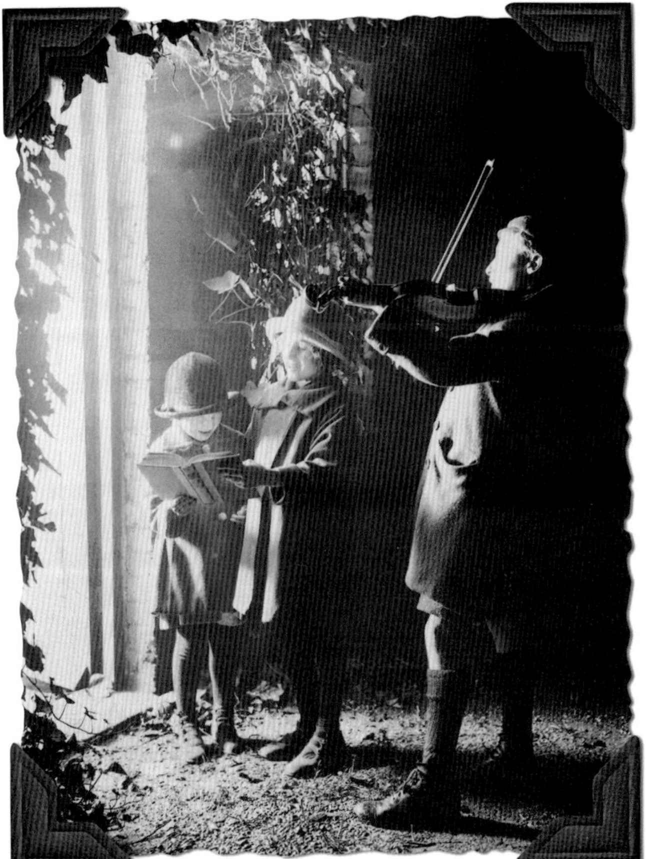

One false move and Miss Prettybox gets a cardboard spike through the throat.

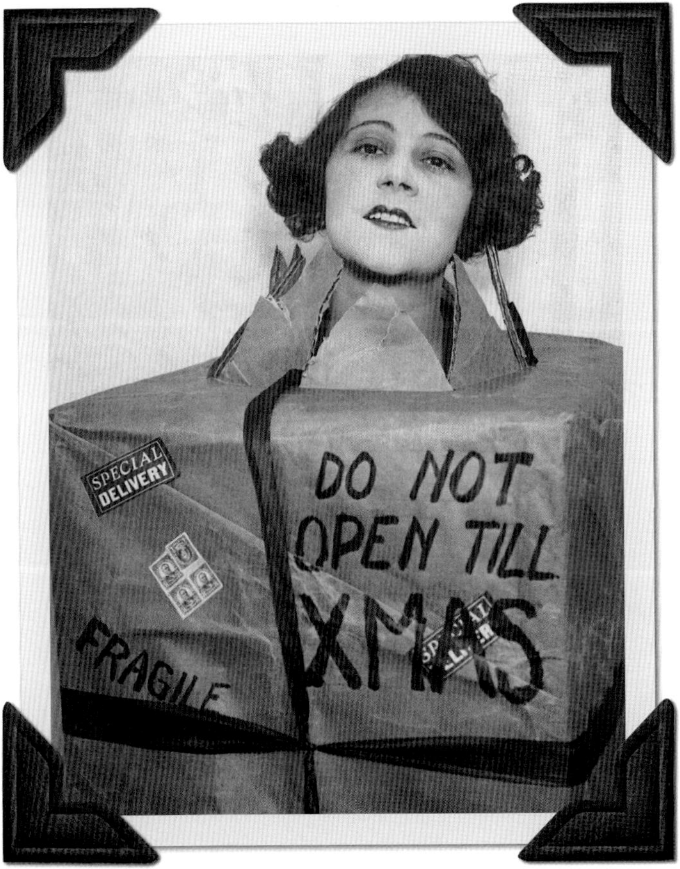
SPECIAL
DELIVERY
DO NOT
OPEN TILL
XMAS
FRAGILE

Yes, Virginia. You do make us feel horny.

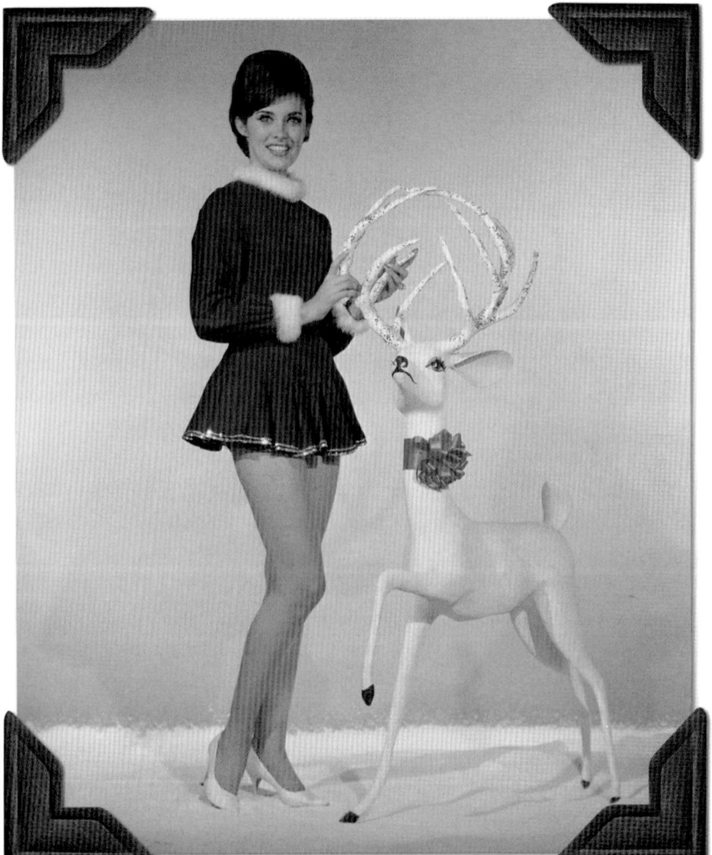

As choir director, Father Arnold spent countless hours training the boys to produce full-throated, round tones. No special reason.

POPULAR CHRISTMAS ANTHEMS and CAROLS
O holy night
ADOLPHE ADAM

Excuse me, *Miss Thang* . . . are you deaf or just a stone-cold bitch? I *asked* who does your hair.

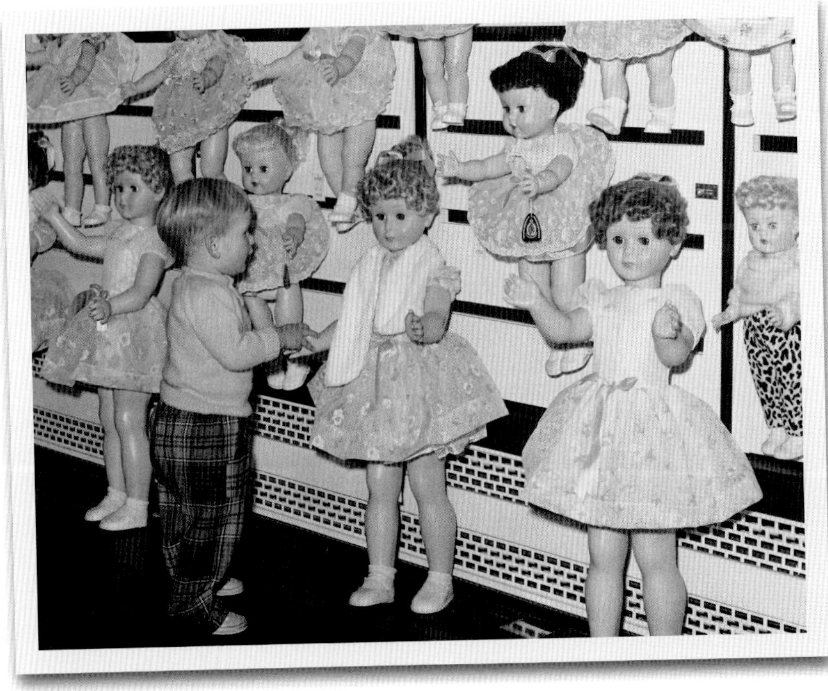

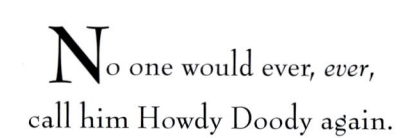

No one would ever, *ever*, call him Howdy Doody again.

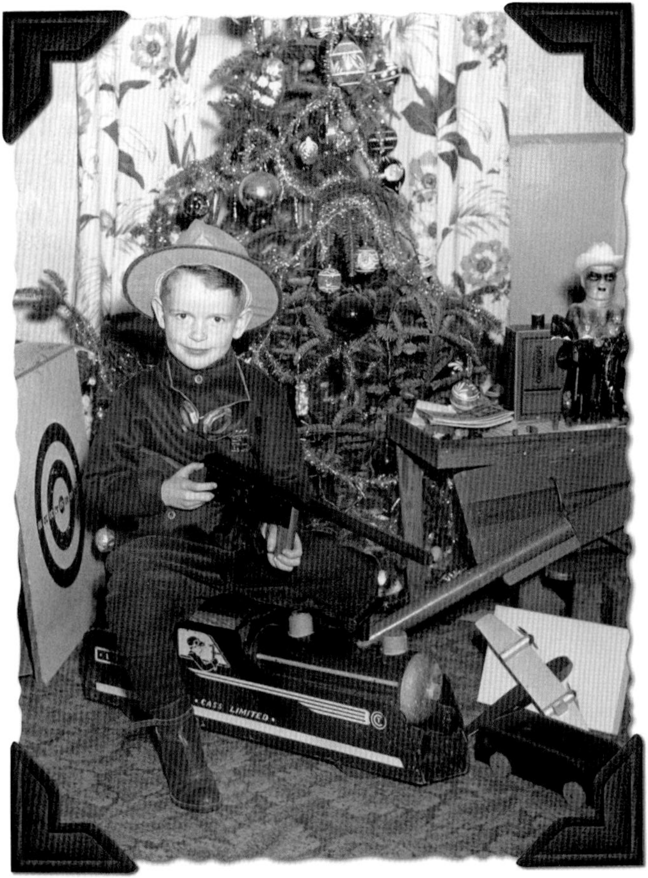
CASS LIMITED

Okay, kiddies. Here we are at Santa's workshop. See all the jolly little elves making Santa's toys and sprinkling fairy dust over everything? Yes. It's a magical place. Merry Christmas from Santa's sweat . . . uh, workshop, kiddies.

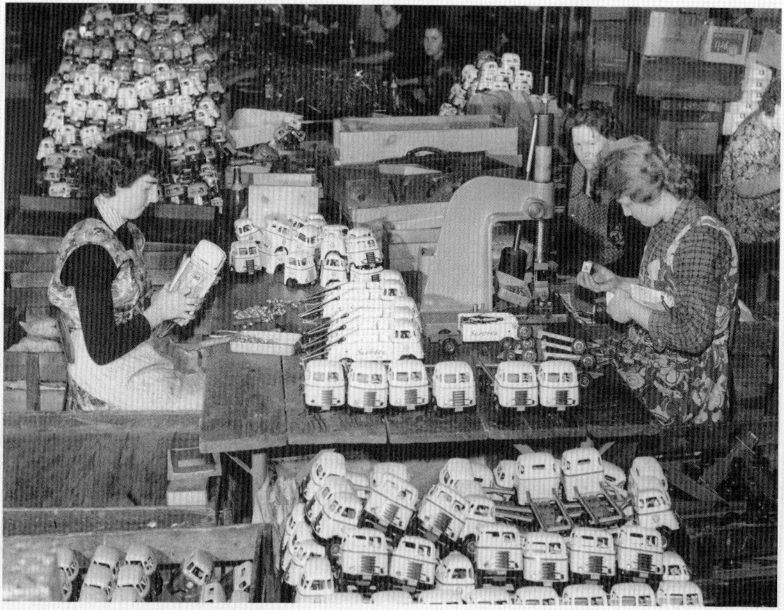

Stupid, lucky, sick war orphans—
they get all the special treatment.

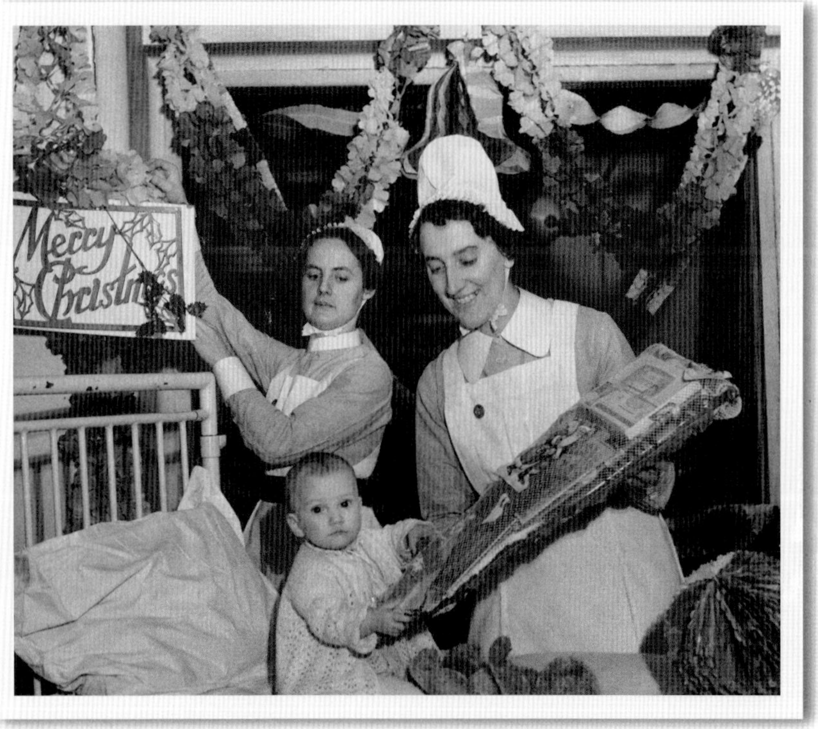
Merry Christmas

On Dimples! On Vixen!

On Sweet Cheeks!

Santa's late for happy hour!

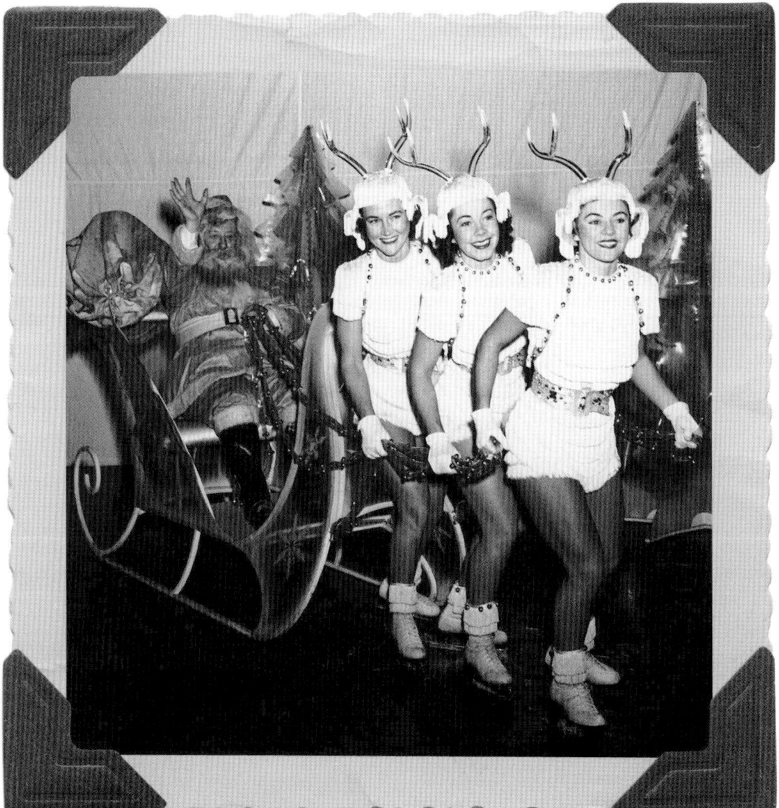

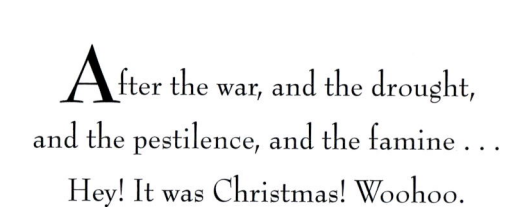

After the war, and the drought, and the pestilence, and the famine . . . Hey! It was Christmas! Woohoo.

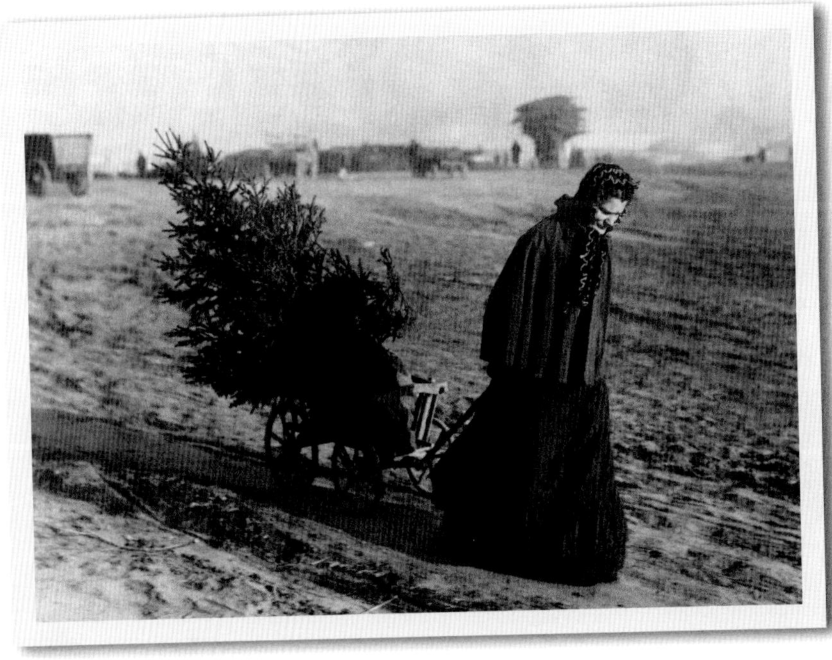

Ultimately, Diddle the Elf had to be let go for conducting inappropriate "testing" of the finished products.

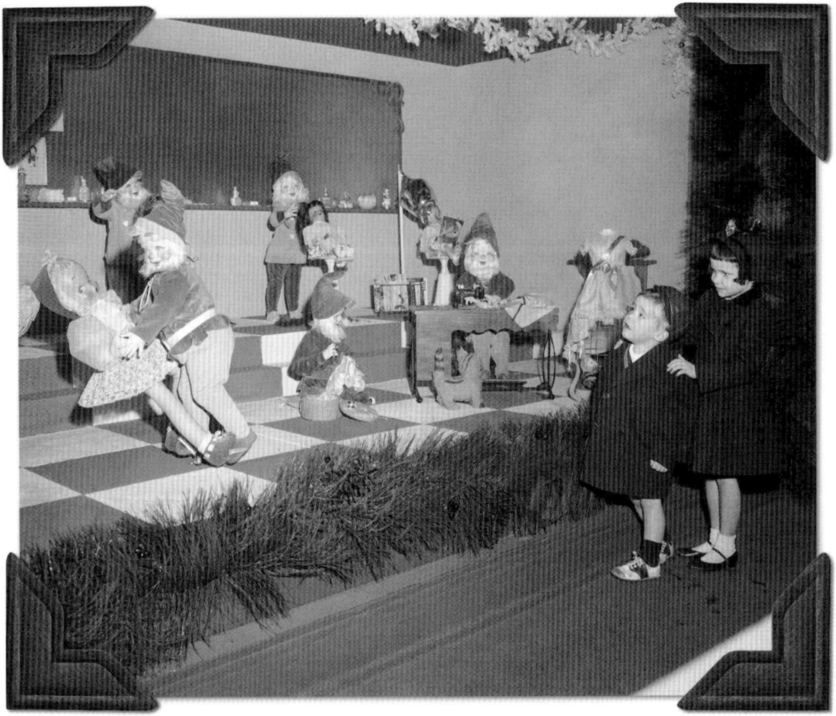

In the end, it was the child support payments that drove Santa to ruin. Turns out the whole "comes but once a year" thing was way off.

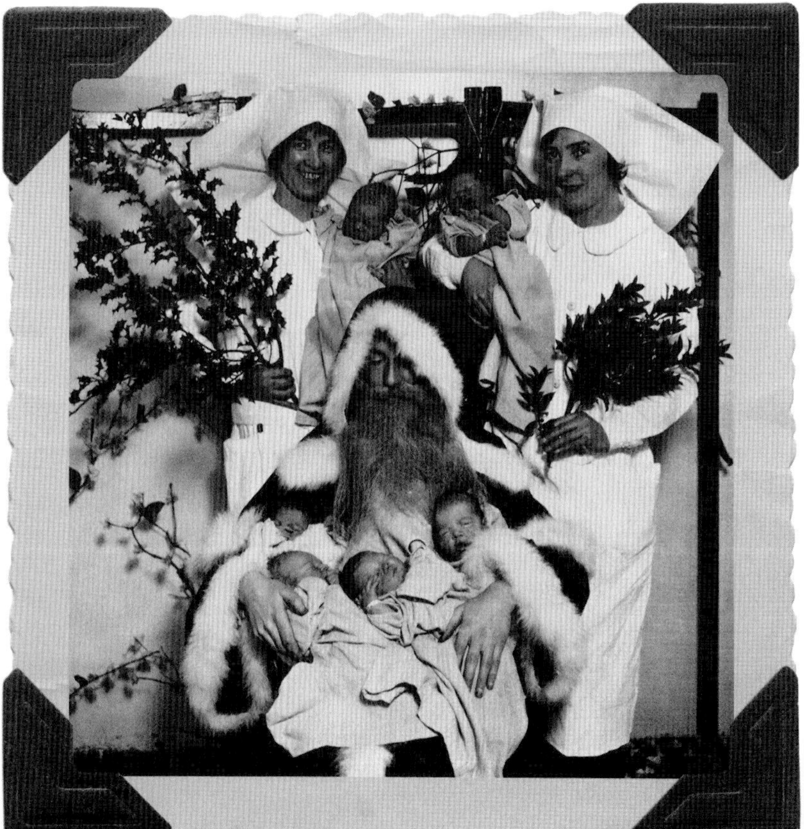

W hoops. Wrong book.

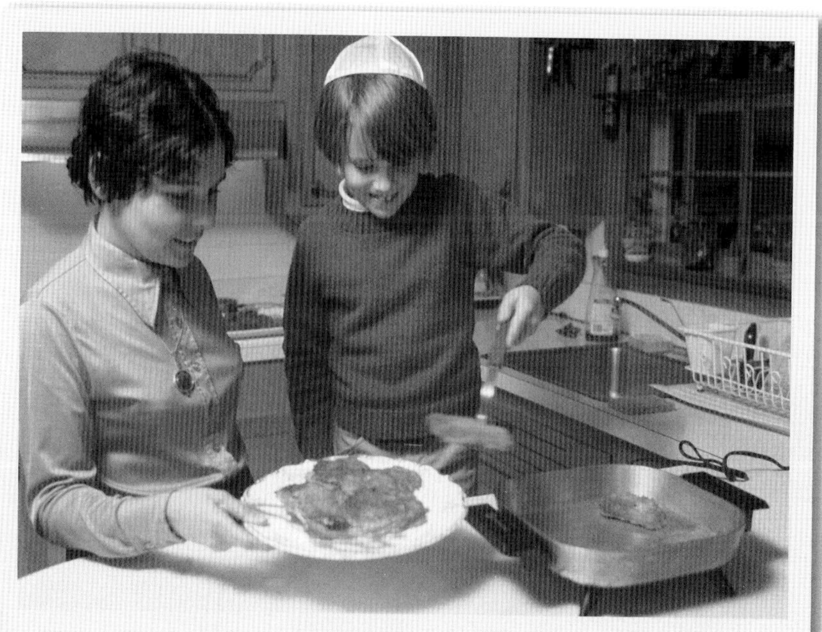

Baked football for Christmas dinner.

God bless us every one!

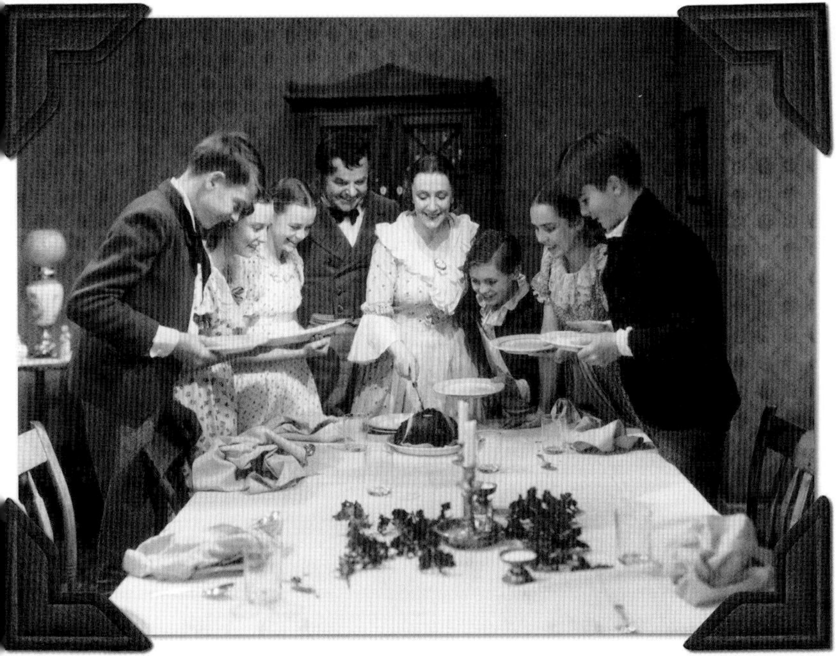

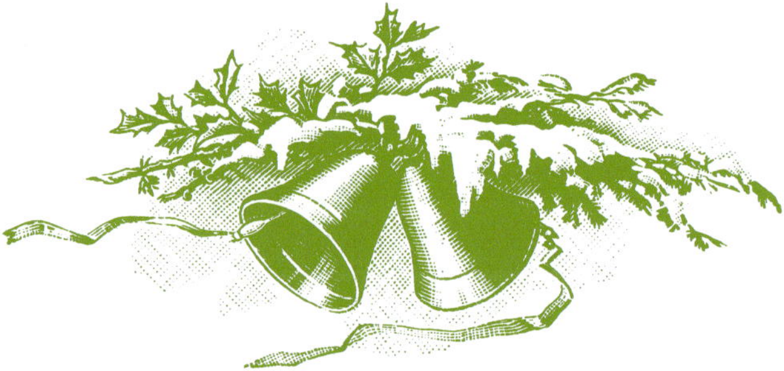